The Jolly

77 songs – folk and pop

chosen by Roger Bush
drawings by Roy Bentley

WORDS EDITION

A & C Black · London

First published 1980
by A & C Black (Publishers) Ltd
35 Bedford Row, London WC1R 4JH

Reprinted 1982, 1983, 1985, 1990, 1993, 1995.

ISBN 0 7136 2096 X
© 1980 A & C Black (Publishers) Ltd

A music edition (ISBN 0 7136 2094 3) is available.

Printed in Great Britain by
Martins the Printers Ltd, Berwick upon Tweed

Contents

Some of the tales are a little unlikely . . .

. . . but there's no shortage of great old stories.

The country folk sit in one corner . . .

. . . and the matelots in another.

The old heartaches ache once more ...

... but our host, preferring a cheerful atmosphere, interrupts with "Have a round on me" ...

... and then gets us together for some old favourites ...

... to all of which we can only say ...

1 The Jolly Herring

1   Now what will I do with my herring's head?
Aye, what will I do with my herring's head?
I'll make it into loaves of bread.
    Herring's head? Loaves of bread?
Aye, and all manner of things.

      Of all the fish that live in the sea
      The herring is the one for me.
      Well, what do you say to such a thing?
      Have I done well with my jolly herring?

2   Now what will I do with my herring's eyes?
Aye, what will I do with my herring's eyes?
I'll make them into puddings and pies.
    Herring's eyes? Puddings and pies?
    Herring's head? Loaves of bread?
Aye, and all manner of things.
    Of all the fish that live in the sea . . .

3   Now what will I do with my herring's gills?
Aye, what will I do with my herring's gills?
I'll make them into window sills.
    Herring's gills? Window sills?
    Herring's eyes? Puddings and pies?
    Herring's head? Loaves of bread?
Aye, and all manner of things.
    Of all the fish that live in the sea . . .

4   Now what will I do with my herring's back?
Aye, what will I do with my herring's back?
I'll make it into a fishing smack.
> Herring's back? Fishing smack?
> Herring's gills? Window sills?
> Herring's eyes? Puddings and pies?
> Herring's head? Loaves of bread?
Aye, and all manner of things.
> Of all the fish that live in the sea . . .

5   Now what will I do with my herring's fins?
Aye, what will I do with my herring's fins?
I'll make them into needles and pins.
> Herring's fins? Needles and pins? . . .
> Of all the fish that live in the sea . . .

6   Now what will I do with my herring's tail?
Aye, what will I do with my herring's tail?
I'll make it into a barrel of ale.
> Herring's tail? Barrel of ale? . . .
> Of all the fish that live in the sea . . .

traditional

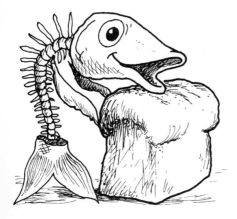

2 The mountain dew

1 Let grasses grow and the waters flow
  in a free and easy way,
But give me enough of the rare old stuff
  that's made near Galway Bay.
And policemen all from Donegal,
  Sligo and Leitrim too,
We'll give them the slip and we'll take a sip
  of the real old mountain dew.

  Hi the diddle-y-I-dillum diddle-y doodle-I-dillum
  Diddle-y doo-ri diddle-y-di day,
  Hi the diddle-y-I-dillum diddle-y doodle-I-dillum
  Diddle-y doo-ri diddle-y-di day.

2 At the foot of the hill there's a neat little still
  where the smoke curls up to the sky.
By the smoke and the smell you can plainly tell
  that there's poteen, boys, nearby,
For it fills the air with a perfume rare,
  and betwixt both me and you,
As home we roll we can drink a bowl
  or a bucket of mountain dew.

3 Now learned men who use the pen
  have wrote the praises high
Of the sweet poteen from Ireland green,
  distilled from wheat and rye.
Away with pills, it will cure all ills,
  for pagan, Christian or Jew,
So take off your coat and grease your throat
  with the real old mountain dew.

traditional

3 The gulls o' Invergordon

1 In Invergordon by the sea
     they've built a new distillery,
  And all the gulls are on the spree
     that live in Invergordon.
  The mash that's flowing from the still
     they gobble down wi' right good will
  And every gull can hold his gill
     that lives in Invergordon.

> Dirumadoo-a-dirumaday
> Dirumadoo-a-daddy-o,
> Dirumadoo-a-dirumaday
> The gulls o' Invergordon.

2 A Glesca gull came from the Clyde
     in Invergordon to reside,
  He got himself half stupefied
     wi' the gulls o' Invergordon.
  And then he found to his surprise
     that he was hardly fit to rise
  And flying kind of side-a-wise
     when he left Invergordon.

3 Now when we die some people say
     we come back in some other shape.
  Oh, how I'd like to come and stay
     as a gull in Invergordon.
  Dirumadoo-a-dirumaday,
     reincarnation would be gay,
  A kind o' perpetual Hogmanay
     wi' the gulls o' Invergordon.

Glesca: Glasgow

4 Right said Fred

1   "Right" said Fred,
    "Both of us together,
    One each end and steady as we go."
    Tried to shift it,
    Couldn't even lift it,
    We were getting nowhere,
    And so we had a cuppa tea, and

    "Right" said Fred,
    "Give a shout for Charlie."
    Up comes Charlie from the floor below.
    After straining,
    Heaving and complaining,
    We was getting nowhere,
    And so we had a cuppa tea,

        And Charlie had a think,
        And he thought we ought
        To take off all the handles,
        And the things wot held the candles,
        But it did no good,
        Well, I never thought it would.

    "All right" said Fred,
    "Have to take the feet off,
    To get them feet off wouldn't take a mo."
    Took its feet off,
    Even took the seat off,
    Should have got us somewhere, but no.
    So Fred said "Let's have another cuppa tea."
    And we said "Right-o."

2 "Right" said Fred,
   "Have to take the door off,
   Need more space to shift the so-and-so."
   Had bad twinges
   Taking off the hinges,
   And it got us nowhere,
   And so we had a cuppa tea, and

   "Right" said Fred,
   "Have to take the wall down,
   That there wall is gonna have to go."
   Took the wall down,
   Even with it all down
   We was getting nowhere
   And so we had a cuppa tea,

        And Charlie had a think,
        And he said "Look, Fred,
        I got a sort of feeling,
        If we remove the ceiling,
        With a rope or two
        We could drop the blighter through."

   "All right" said Fred,
   Climbing up a ladder,
   With his crowbar gave a mighty blow.
   Was he in trouble,
   Half a ton of rubble
   Landed on the top of his dome.
   Charlie and me had another cuppa tea,
   And then we went home.

Spoken: I said to Charlie "We'll just have to leave it
standing on the landing, that's all." Trouble with Fred is,
he's too hasty. Never get nowhere if you're too hasty . . .

Myles Rudge

5 Hole in the ground

1   There I was digging this hole,
    Hole in the ground, so big and sorta round it was,
    And there was I digging it deep,
    It was flat at the bottom and the sides were steep,
    When along comes this bloke in a bowler
    Which he lifted and scratched his head,
    Oh, he looked in the hole, poor demented soul,
    And said:

    "Don't dig it there, dig it elsewhere,
    It shouldn't be round, it ought to be square.
    The shape of it's wrong, it's much too long,
    And you can't put a hole where a hole don't belong."

2   There was I stood in my hole,
    Shovelling earth for all that I was worth I was,
    And there was him standing up there,
    So grand and official with his nose in the air,
    So I gave him a look sort of sideways,
    And I leaned on my shovel and sighed,
    Oh, I lit me a fag, and having took a drag,
    Replied:

    "Just couldn't bear to dig it elsewhere,
    I'm digging it round 'cos I don't want it square.
    If you disagree, doesn't bother me,
    'Cos this is the place where the hole's gonna be."

3   There we were discussing this hole,
    Hole in the ground, so big and sorta round it was,
    It's not there now, the ground's all flat,
    And beneath it is the bloke in the bowler hat.
    And that's that.

    Myles Rudge

6 Drill, ye tarriers, drill

1 Every morning at seven o'clock
There are twenty tarriers drilling at the rock
And the boss comes round and says "Keep still,
And come down heavy on the cast-iron drill."

  And drill, ye tarriers, drill,
  Drill, ye tarriers, drill.
  Well, you work all day for the sugar in your tay,
  Down behind the railway,
  And drill, ye tarriers, drill. And blast. And fire.

2 Now our new foreman was Gene McCann,
By golly he was a blinken man.
Last week a premature blast went off,
And a mile in the air went Big Jim Goff.
  And drill, ye tarriers, drill . . .

3 Next time payday comes around
Jim Goff a dollar short was found,
When asked what for, got this reply:
"You were docked for the time you were up in the sky."
  And drill, ye tarriers, drill . . .

4 Now the boss was a fine man down to the ground
And he married a lady six feet round,
She baked good bread, and she baked it well,
But she baked it hard as the holes in —
  And drill, ye tarriers, drill . . .

Thomas F. Casey

7 Indeed I would

1   As I went out through Camden Town, up came
    a Murphy truck,
    And a gombeen man he said to me "Would you
    like to shift some muck?"

> O indeed I would
> Don't you know I would,
> With me right fol del the diddle-do,
> Indeed I would.

2   He got me by the collar and he dropped me
    on the floor,
    There was fifty Tipperary men and from Galway
    twenty more,

> O indeed there was
> Don't you know there was . . .

3   We raced along the road until the ganger gave
    a shout,
    "Get down into the trench, me boys, and start
    to throw it out."

> O indeed he did
> Don't you know he did . . .

4   I grabbed me pick and shovel and I started
    for to dig,
    And the fella right in front of me was grunting
    like a pig,

> O indeed he was
> Don't you know he was . . .

5 Says I "If you keep on like that you'll be dying
    for the job."
The ganger man he heard me and he shouted "Shut
    your gob."
        O indeed he did
        Don't you know he did . . .

6 The ganger came from Skibbereen, he'd been
    a drover then,
Instead of driving cattle now he works at driving
    men,
        O indeed he does
        Don't you know he does . . .

7 Now here's a piece of good advice, it is the golden
    rule,
When they call you a good worker, it's a nickname
    for a fool.
        O indeed it is
        Don't you know it is . . .

gombeen man: an extortionate middleman

Ewan MacColl

8 Settle-Carlisle railway

1 In the year of '69 they planned to run a train
From Settle to Carlisle all across the mountain range.
They employed three thousand navvies to build this
   mighty road,
And across the fells to Appleby that old steam engine
   rolled.

> And it's:
> Up in the morning, lads, in wind, snow or hail,
> Hold fast to your hammers, lads, and lay another
>   rail.

2 It's 72 miles from Settle to Carlisle,
Across the roughest country in the British Isles.
They said it would take four years but it took them
   nearer seven,
And the first twenty miles sent four hundred men
   to heaven.

3 And when the winter came it froze them to the floor,
It blew them off the viaducts and it killed them
   on Blea Moor.
Some died of the smallpox and some of cholera;
Chapal and St Leonards have many buried there.

4 So if you ride this famous line across the heathered
   fells,
When crossing Ribblehead Viaduct remember the tale
   I tell.
There's Mallerstang and Aisgill and the Dent Dale's
   lovely wilds,
And navvy-lads a-slaving from Settle to Carlisle.

Mike Donald

9 Coal-hole cavalry

1   Early morning, dreaming is shattered,
    One clitter-clatter on t' flags outside,
    Old knocker-upper rat-tatting on t' window,
    Making sure nobody's o'er-lied.

> Clittering, clattering, coal-hole cavalry,
> Galloping, rain or fine,
> Clittering, clattering, coal-hole cavalry,
> Galloping down to t' mine.

2   Father yawning, drizzle on t' window,
    More clitter-clattering coming down th'hill,
    Stairs are creaking, oven door banging,
    Father waiting for Uncle Bill.

3   Mam is filling 'is bottle wi' water,
    Clatter-clitter-clatter and a rattle on t' latch.
    Clogs in t' lobby and talking quiet,
    Arguing t' toss about Sunday's match.

4   Come on, Billy lad, best get going,
    Clatter-clitter-clatter an' t' front door bang,
    Going down to t' mucky old coal-pit,
    Hear t' pit-hat and snap-tin clang.

5   Colliers riding a million horses,
    Clatter-clitter-clatter all over t' world.
    Look out, Injuns! Cavalry's coming,
    Picks and shovels and banners unfurled.

6   Buzzer's blowing a sound of victory,
    Clatter-clitter-clattering's over and done.
    All t' world's quiet and sleep is coming,
    Wish I were a collier, it must be fun.

Ted Edwards

10 This old hammer

1   This old hammer killed John Henry
    This old hammer killed John Henry
    This old hammer killed John Henry
    But it won't kill me, won't kill me.

2   This old hammer shines like silver
    This old hammer shines like silver
    This old hammer shines like silver
    But it rings like gold, rings like gold.

3   This old hammer killed John Henry
    This old hammer killed John Henry
    This old hammer killed John Henry
    But it won't kill me, won't kill me.

    traditional

11 The broadside man

1   There are floods in Worcester Town
    And the rain is tumbling down
    And a most amazing monster has been captured in the
        Dee.
    Here's a bold and stirring tale
    Of the hunting of the whale
    And the story of a parson who was pressed away to sea.

>   Come and buy, come and buy,
>   Be you poor or genterye,
>   Gather round the broadside man and pay your
>   money down.
>   Ballads long and short
>   And the best of every sort,
>   For a single paltry penny all the news of London
>   Town.

2   Here's the finest sheets of all,
    Fresh today from Stationers' Hall,
    A newly-written ballad of Lord Nelson's victory.
    Here's the news from all the courts,
    Of the cases and reports,
    And the rantings of a pirate who was hanged on
        Tyburn Tree.

3   Here's the story of a maid
    Of the brisk and rambling trade,
    Deceiving of a tinker who was taken by her charms,
    And the story of a wife,
    It's the truth upon my life,
    Who came upon her husband rolling in the milkmaid's
        arms.

John Conolly and Bill Meek

12 Timothy Winters

1   Timothy Winters comes to school
    With eyes as wide as a football pool,
    Ears like bombs and teeth like splinters:
    A blitz of a boy is Timothy Winters.

2   His belly is white, his neck is dark,
    And his hair is an exclamation mark.
    His clothes are enough to scare a crow
    And through his britches the blue winds blow.

3   When teacher talks he won't hear a word
    And he shoots down dead the arithmetic-bird,
    He licks the patterns off his plate
    And he's not even heard of the Welfare State.

4   Timothy Winters has bloody feet
    And he lives in a house on Suez Street,
    He sleeps in a sack on the kitchen floor
    And they say there aren't boys like him any more.

5   Old Man Winters likes his beer
    And his missus ran off with a bombardier,
    Grandma sits in the grate with a gin
    And Timothy's dosed with an aspirin.

6   The Welfare Worker lies awake
    But the law's as tricky as a ten-foot snake,
    So Timothy Winters drinks his cup
    And slowly goes on growing up.

7   At Morning Prayers the Master helves
    For children less fortunate than ourselves,
    And the loudest response in the room is when
    Timothy Winters roars "Amen!"

8 So come one angel, come on ten:
Timothy Winters says "Amen
Amen amen amen amen."
Timothy Winters, Lord.

Amen.

Charles Causley

13 Pete was a lonely mongrel dog who lived in central Wigan, Lancs

1   Pete was a lonely mongrel dog
        who lived in central Wigan.
    He had a great thought one winter's day
        while out for bones a-digging:
    He'd change his life and he'd change his ways
        and a sailor-man he'd be,
    So he packed his tail and buried his bones
        and off to sea went he.

            Off to sea went, off to sea went,
                off to sea went he-e-e,
            Off to sea went, off to sea went,
                off to sea went he.

2   He joined an English man-o'-war
        as first mate to the captain,
    They travelled far to many lands
        where the trees were tall and champion.
    He roamed the seas until he found
        it wasn't what he'd dreamed:
    There was no place to bury his bones
        and his tail was a permanent green.
    He'd change his life and he'd change his ways
        and a soldier he would be,
    So he buried his bones in the ocean deep
        and off to war went he.

            Off to war went, off to war went,
                off to war went he-e-e,
            Off to war went, off to war went,
                off to war went he.

3   He joined the Royal Artillery
        as mascot to the battery.
    Well he combed his hair and polished his tail
        and did things very exactly.
    Well they marched him up and down the square
        and stood him to attention,
    But when he'd chased the cook-house cat
        they put him in detention.
    He'd change his life and he'd change his ways
        and an airman he would be,
    So he swapped his guns for a set of wings
        and off to fly went he.

            Off to fly went, off to fly went,
                off to fly went he-e-e,
            Off to fly went, off to fly went,
                off to fly went he.

4   He joined the Royal flying lads
        as assistant navigator;
    At finding his way from here to there
        there never was anyone greater.
    He flew through the air at incredible speeds
        and sometimes upside-down,
    And after a while he thought it was
        much safer on the ground.
    He'd change his life and he'd change his ways
        and go back to his digging,
    So he packed his tail and left his bones
        and sniffed his way to Wigan.
    He'd change his life and he'd change his ways
        and he'd go back to his digging,
    And spend his days in simple ways:
        with his tail 'neath the trees of Wigan.

John Meeks and Colin Radcliffe

14 Bob the pedigree sheepdog

1   I've got a dog, his name is Bob,
And I know he's a pedigree sheepdog,
'Cos if walkers stray on the Pennine Way
He'll prove he's a Dales-bred sheepdog,
And he'll fill the pen with assorted men,
Something to sharpen his teeth on,
And his picnic taste for salmon paste
Proves he's a Dales-bred sheepdog.

2   Now at sheepdog trials they come for miles
Just to see a pedigree sheepdog,
And his country fans all clap their hands
'Cos they know he's a Dales-bred sheepdog.
Whilst others leap to round up sheep
He's a nowhere-to-be-seen dog;
Knocking down Newcastle Brown
Proves he's a pint-size sheepdog.

3   Now cars and bikes and folks on hikes
Are clogging all the Dales up,
And if it goes on there won't be none
For our littermen to clean up.
But Bob works hard in his own farmyard,
He doesn't need a reason;
A tourist a day keeps pollution away,
And it's always open season.

4 A dog-food man with a can in his hand
   Full of marrowbone jelly and noodles,
   Said he's had enough of dogs from Crufts
   And temperamental poodles.
   He could take us far, make Bob a star:
   Gold-plated kennels and houses.
   But Bob gave a grin as he opened the tin
   And took the backside out of his trousers.

5 Now a man came round from the Skipton Pound,
   In his hand he carried a summons,
   'Cos Bob put a paw outside the law,
   By gum, he is a rum 'un!
   They'd had complaints to use restraints
   And swore out an injuncture:
   Bob's offence was he'd no licence
   To practise acupuncture.
          So if you see Bob, the outlaw dog,
          Better leave him well alone,
          'Cos he likes little girls with long blonde curls
          Much better than a bone.

Mike Donald and Roger Chappell

15 Football crazy

1   I have a favourite brother
     and his christian name is Paul,
He's lately joined a football club
     for he's mad about football.
He's two black eyes already,
     and teeth lost from his gob,
Since Paul became a member
     of that terrible football club.

     For he's football crazy, he's football mad,
       The football it has taken away
         the little bit of sense he had.
       And it would take a dozen servants
         to wash his clothes and scrub,
       Since Paul became a member
         of that terrible football club.

2   In the middle of the field, one afternoon,
     the captain says, "Now Paul,
Would you kindly take this place-kick
     since you're mad about football?"
So he took forty paces backwards,
     shot off from the mark,
The ball went sailing over the bar
     and landed in New Yark.

3   His wife she says she'll leave him
     if Paulie doesn't keep
Away from football kicking
     at night-time in his sleep;
He calls out "Pass, McGinty"
     and other things so droll,
Last night he kicked her out of bed
     and swore it was a goal!

traditional

16 Cotton Jenny

1 There's a house on a hill,
   By a worn-down weathered old mill,
   In the valley below where the river winds,
   There's no such thing as bad times,
   And a soft southern flame,
   O, Cotton Jenny's her name,
   She wakes me up when the sun goes down,
   And the wheels of love go round,
     Wheels of love go round, love go round,
     Love go round, a joyful sound.
     I ain't got a penny
     For Cotton Jenny
     To spend,
     But then the wheels go round.

2 When the new day begins
   I go down to the cotton gin,
   And I make my time worth while to them,
   Then I climb back up again.
   And she waits by the door,
   "O Cotton Jenny, I'm sore."
   She rubs my feet while the sun goes down,
   And the wheels of love go round,

3 In the hot sickly south,
   When they say, "Well shut ma mouth,"
   I can never be free from the cotton grind,
   But I know what's mine.
   A soft southern flame,
   O, Cotton Jenny's her name,
   She wakes me up when the sun goes down,
   And the wheels of love go round,

Gordon Lightfoot

17 Leave them a flower

1   I speak on behalf of the next generation,
     My sons and my daughters, their children to come.
     What will you leave them for their recreation?
     An oil slick, a pylon, an industrial slum?

         Leave them a flower, some grass and a hedgerow,
         A hill and a valley, a view to the sea.
         These things are not yours to destroy as you want to,
         A gift given once for eternity.

2   You plunder, you pillage, you tear and you tunnel,
     Trees lying toppled, roots finger the sky.
     Building a land for machines and computers.
     In the name of progress the farms have to die.
         Leave them a flower, some grass and a hedgerow . . .

3   Fish in an ocean polluted and poisoned,
     The sand on the beaches is stinking and black.
     You with your tankers, your banks and investments
     Say "Never worry, the birds will come back."
         Leave them a flower, some grass and a hedgerow . . .

4   When the last flower has dropped its last petal,
     When the last concrete is finally laid,
     The moon will shine cold on a nightmarish landscape,
     Your gift to our children, the world which you've made.
         Leave them a flower, some grass and a hedgerow . . .

Wally Whyton

18 Across the hills

1

voice A Across the hills black clouds are sweeping,
Carry poison far and wide,
And the grass has blackened underfoot,
And the rose has withered and died.

voice B But the rose is still as red, love,
    and the grass is still as green,
And it must have been a shadow
    in the distance you have seen,
Yes, it must have been a shadow you have seen.

2

voice A But can't you hear the children weeping?
Can't you hear the mournful sound?
And no birds sing in the twisted trees
In the silent streets around.

voice B I can hear the children laughing
    in the streets as they play,
And you must have caught the dying
    of an echo far away,
Yes, it must have been an echo far away.

3

voice A But can't you see the white ash falling
From the hollow of the skies?
And the blood runs red down the blackened walls
Where a ruined city lies.

voice B I can see the red sun shining
    in the park on the stream,
And you must have felt a shiver
    from the darkness of a dream,
Yes, it must have been the darkness of a dream.

4

voice A And death shall reap a hellish harvest,
               Make a desert of this land.
voice B But the rose is still as red, love,
                  and the grass is still as green,
               And it must have been a shadow you have seen.
               Yes, the rose is still as red, love,
                  and the grass is still as green,
               And it must have been a shadow you have seen.

Leon Rosselson

Leon Rosselson, who wrote this song, tells us, "The attitudes of the two voices are intended to be complementary rather than contradictory – I wasn't taking sides. Together, they seem to me to represent a more complete awareness – of the possibilities of life and the possibility of its destruction."

19 Pollution

1 If you visit American city
You will find it very pretty.
Just two things of which you must beware:
Don't drink the water and don't breathe the air.

> Pollution, pollution, they got smog and sewage and
> mud,
> Turn on your tap and get hot and cold running crud.

2 See the halibuts and the sturgeons
Being wiped out by detergeons.
Fish gotta swim and birds gotta fly,
But they don't last long if they try.

> Pollution, pollution, you can use the latest toothpaste,
> And then rinse your mouth with industrial waste.

3 Just go out for a breath of air,
And you'll be ready for Medicare.
The city streets are really quite a thrill,
If the hoods don't get you, the monoxide will.

> Pollution, pollution, wear a gas-mask and a veil,
> Then you can breathe, long as you don't inhale.

4 Lots of things there that you can drink,
But stay away from the kitchen sink,
Throw out your breakfast garbage and I've got a hunch
That the folks down-stream will drink it for lunch.

> So go to the city, see the crazy people there,
> Like lambs to the slaughter
> They're drinking the water
> And breathing (*cough . . . splutter*) the air.

Tom Lehrer

20 Air

Welcome, sulphur dioxide,
Hello, carbon monoxide,
The air, the air is everywhere.
Breathe deep while you sleep, breathe deep.

Bless you, alcohol blood stream,
Save me, nicotine lung steam,
Incense, incense is in the air.
Breathe deep while you sleep, breathe deep.

Cataclysmic ectoplasm,
Fall-out atomic orgasm,
Vapour and fume, at the stone of my tomb,
Breathing like a sullen perfume,
Eating at the stone of my tomb.

Welcome, sulphur dioxide,
Hello, carbon monoxide,
The air, the air is everywhere.
Breathe deep while you sleep, breathe deep (*cough*)
    deep (*cough*) deep de deep (*cough*).

James Rado and Gerome Ragni

21 My last cigarette

1   Tobacco, tobacco, I hate you I do,
Like Tarzan I'd look if it wasn't for you.
   But I'll give up the habit, I will even yet,
   When I've had just one more cigarette.
It wasn't the whisky, it wasn't the wine
That made such a wreck of this body of mine,
   But I'll give up the habit, I will even yet,
   When I've had just one more cigarette.

2   Under my eyes are a couple of bags,
I blame it all on to a packet of fags,
   But I'll give up the habit, I will even yet,
   When I've had just one more cigarette.
My teeth are all yellow and so is my tongue,
I breathe through a kipper, I call it a lung,
   But I'll give up the habit, I will even yet,
   When I've had just one more cigarette.

3   Nail in my coffin so pale and so thin,
I am a fool to keep driving you in.
   You say that you'll kill me, how much do you bet?
   When I've had just one more cigarette.
I'll fling the packet away, away,
Fifty times in a week I say,
   Fling the packet away, away,
   When I've had just one more cigarette.

Sydney Carter

22 I'm the urban spaceman

I'm the urban spaceman, baby, I've got speed,
I've got everything I need.
I'm the urban spaceman, baby, I can fly,
I'm a supersonic guy.
I don't need pleasure, I don't feel pain,
If you were to knock me down I'd just get up again,
I'm the urban spaceman, I've got hairs on my chest,
I never get depressed.

I wake up every morning with a smile upon my face,
My natural exuberance spills out all over the place.
I'm the urban spaceman, baby, I'm making out,
I'm all about.

I'm the urban spaceman, I'm intelligent and keen,
Know what I mean?
I'm the urban spaceman, as a lover second to none,
It's a lot of fun.
I never let my friends down, I've never made a boob,
I'm a glossy magazine, an advert in the tube,
I'm the urban spaceman, baby, here comes the twist:
I don't exist.

Neil Innes

23 Colonel Fazackerley

1   Colonel Fazackerley Butterworth-Toast
    Bought an old castle complete with a ghost,
    But someone or other forgot to declare
    To Colonel Fazack that the spectre was there.

2   On the very first evening, while waiting to dine,
    The Colonel was taking a fine sherry wine,
    When the ghost, with a furious flash and a flare,
    Shot out of the chimney and shivered, "Beware!"

3   Colonel Fazackerley put down his glass
    And said, "My dear fellow, that's really first class!
    I just can't conceive how you do it at all.
    I imagine you're going to a Fancy Dress Ball?"

4   At this, the dread ghost gave a withering cry.
    Said the Colonel (his monocle firm in his eye),
    "Now just how you do it I wish I could think.
    Do sit down and tell me, and please have a drink."

5   The ghost in his phosphorous cloak gave a roar
    And floated about between ceiling and floor.
    He walked through a wall and returned through a pane
    And backed up the chimney and came down again.

6   Said the Colonel, "With laughter I'm feeling quite weak!"
    (As trickles of merriment ran down his cheek).
    "My house-warming party I hope you won't spurn.
    You *must* say you'll come and you'll give us a turn!"

7   At this, the poor spectre—quite out of his wits—
    Proceeded to shake himself almost to bits.
    He rattled his chains and he clattered his bones
    And he filled the whole castle with mumbles and moans.

8 But Colonel Fazackerley, just as before,
  Was simply delighted and called out, "Encore!"
  At which the ghost vanished, his efforts in vain,
  And never was seen at the castle again.

9 "Oh dear, what a pity!" said Colonel Fazack.
  "I don't know his name, so I can't call him back."
  And then with a smile that was hard to define,
  Colonel Fazackerley went in to dine.

Charles Causley

24 Where did you get that hat?

1   Now how I came to get this hat, 'tis very strange
     and funny,
  Grandfather died and left to me his property and money;
  And when the will it was read out, they told me straight
     and flat,
  If I would have his money, I must always wear his hat!

  Spoken: And everywhere I go, everyone shouts at me:

     "Where did you get that hat?
     Where did you get that tile?
     Isn't it a nobby one, and just the proper style?
     I should like to have one just the same as that!"
     Where'er I go they shout "Hello! Where did you get
       that hat?"

2   If I go to the op'ra house, in the op'ra season,
  There's someone sure to shout at me without the
     slightest reason.
  If I go to a concert hall to have a jolly spree,
  There's someone in the party who is sure to shout at me:
     "Where did you get that hat? . . .

3   At twenty-one I thought I would to my sweetheart
     get married,
  The people in the neighbourhood had said too long
     we'd tarried.
  So off to church we went right quick, determined
     to get wed;
  I had not long been in there when the parson to me
     said:
     "Where did you get that hat? . . .

4 I once tried hard to be MP but failed to get elected,
Upon a tub I stood, round which a thousand folks
   collected;
And I had dodged the eggs and bricks (which was no
   easy task),
When one man cried, "A question I the candidate would
   ask!"

Spoken: I told him that I was ready to reply to any question that could be put to me. The man said: "Thousands of British working people are anxiously awaiting enlightenment on the subject on which I am about to address you. It is a question of national importance, in fact: THE great problem of the day—and that is, Sir:
    Where did you get that hat? . . .

5 When Colonel South, the millionaire, gave his last
   garden party,
I was among the guests who had a welcome true
   and hearty;
The Prince of Wales was also there, and my heart
   jumped with glee
When I was told the Prince would like to have a word
   with me.

Spoken: I was immediately presented to His Royal Highness who immediately exclaimed:
    "Where did you get that hat? . . .

Charles Rolmas

25 The Field of the Willows

1   In the Field of the Willows where I used to stay
    'Twas there that I washed all my troubles away
    With the rain coming down every hour of the day
    In the Field of the Willows so gay.

2   I saw an old man looking awfully queer
    Sat under a tree with a bottle of beer
    But when I got there he'd been dead for a year
    In the Field of the Willows so gay.

3   To leave him unburied I knew was a sin
    But I was too lazy a grave to begin
    So I put on my boots and I trampled him in
    In the Field of the Willows so gay.

4   As I took a walk by the river one day
    Saw the minister's daughter a-heading my way.
    She said "Come on, let's go and sit down in the hay,"
    In the Field of the Willows so gay.

5   So into the dark of the barn we did creep
    But it wasn't the maiden who sang me to sleep
    But seventeen horses, twelve cows and a sheep
    In the Field of the Willows so gay.

6   There's a hermit lives up on the mountain so high
    And he washes himself every tenth of July.
    The fish in the river roll over and die
    In the Field of the Willows so gay.

7   A dashing young p'liceman went off on his trail
    But he came back next morning all tattered and pale
    With a pitchfork behind like a long wooden tail
    In the Field of the Willows so gay.

8   In the Field of the Willows where I used to stay
    'Twas there that I washed all my troubles away
    With the rain coming down every hour of the day
    In the Field of the Willows so gay.

Dave Goulder

26 Mole in a hole

1   Like the flowers, like the bees,
    Like the woodlands and the trees,
    I like the Byrds and their LPs
    And I'm a refugee.

       Wanna be a mole in a hole,
       Making low and slow,
       Wanna be a fly flying high
       In the sky.
       Wanna be a mole in a hole,
       Making low and slow,
       Wanna be a fly flying high
       In the sky.

2   Well my feet are smelly and my hair's a mess,
    My teeth are yellow and I've got bad breath,
    I may look great but I feel like death
    And I'm a refugee.
       Wanna be a mole in a hole . . .

Mike Waterson

27 Hopalong Peter

1   Old Uncle Peter he got tight,
    Started up to Heaven on a stormy night,
    The road being rough and him not well,
    He lost his way and went to ——

        Hopalong Peter, where are you going?
        Hopalong Peter, where are you going?
        Hopalong Peter, won't you bear in mind
        I ain't coming back till the gooseberry time.

2   Old Mother Hubbard and her dog were Dutch,
    A bow-legged rooster and he hobbled on a crutch,
    Hen chewed tobacco and the duck drank wine,
    The goose played the fiddle on the pumpkin vine.
        Hopalong Peter, where are you going? . . .

3   Down in the barnyard playing seven-up,
    The old tom-cat and the little yellow pup,
    The old Mother Hubbard, she's a-picking out the
        fleas,
    The rooster in the cream jar up to his knees.
        Hopalong Peter, where are you going? . . .

4   I've got a sweet gal in this here town,
    If she weighs an ounce she weighs seven hundred
        pounds,
    Every time my sweet gal turns once around,
    The heel of her shoe makes a hole in the ground.
        Hopalong Peter, where are you going? . . .

traditional

28 MacPherson's farewell

1 Farewell, ye dungeons dark and strong,
  The wretch's destinie!
  MacPherson's time will not be long,
  On yonder gallows-tree.

>   Sae rantingly, sae wantonly,
>   Sae dauntingly gae'd he:
>   He play'd a spring, and danc'd it round
>   Below the gallows-tree.

2 O what is death but parting breath?
  On many'a bloody plain
  I've dared his face, and in this place
  I scorn him yet again!

3 Untie these bands from off my hands,
  And bring to me my sword;
  And there's no a man in all Scotland,
  But I'll brave him at a word.

4 I've liv'd a life of sturt and strife;
  I die by treacherie:
  It burns my heart I must depart
  And not avenged be.

5 Now farewell, light, thou sunshine bright,
  And all beneath the sky!
  May coward shame distain his name,
  The wretch that dares not die!

sae: so
rantingly, wantonly: exultantly, wildly
dauntingly: courageously
gae'd: went
sturt: trouble

Robert Burns

29 Hangman

1 Slack your rope, hangman, slack it for a while,
I think I see my father coming riding many a mile.
Father, have you brought me hope or have you paid
my fee,
Or have you come to see me hanging from the gallows
tree?

> I have not brought you hope,
> I have not paid your fee.
> Yes, I have come to see you hanging
> from the gallows tree.

2 (as verse 1, substituting "mother" for "father")
> I have not brought you hope . . .

3 (as verse 1: "brother")
> I have not brought you hope . . .

4 (as verse 1: "sister")
> I have not brought you hope . . .

5 (as verse 1: "true love")

> Yes, I have brought you hope,
> Yes, I have paid your fee.
> I have not come to see you hanging
> from the gallows tree.

traditional

30 Whiskey in the jar

1   As I was going over Kilgary Mountain
    I met with Captain Farrell and his money he was
      counting.
    First I drew my pistol, and then I drew my sabre,
      saying
    "Stand and deliver, for I am your bold deceiver."

> Wi' my ring-um do-rum day,
> Whack for the daddy-o,
> Whack for my daddy-o,
> There's whiskey in the jar.

2   He counted out his money and it made a pretty penny,
    I loaded up and took it home and gave it to my Jenny.
    She swore that she loved me, that she never would
      deceive me,
    But the devil's in the women and they always lie so easy.

3   I woke next morning early, 'tween the hours of six
      and seven,
    And the guards were standing round the bed in numbers
      odd and even.
    I flew to my pistols but alas I was mistaken,
    For Jenny'd wet the powder and a prisoner I was taken.

4   They threw me into Sligo jail with neither judge nor
      writing,
    For robbing Captain Farrell as he crossed Kilgary
      Mountain,
    But they didn't take my fists and so I knocked the
      jailer down,
    And bid a distant farewell to the judge in Sligo Town.

traditional

31 Turpin hero

1 As Turpin rode across the moor
    He saw a lawyer riding before.
    "Kind sir," says he, "aren't you afraid
    Of Turpin, that mischievous blade?"

        O rare Turpin hero,
        O rare Turpin O.

2 Says Turpin, "He won't find me out,
    I've hid my money in my boot."
    The lawyer says, "No one can find
    The gold stitched in my cape behind."

3 As they rode by the foot of the hill
    Turpin commands him to stand still.
    Says he, "Your cape I must cut off
    For my mare she needs a new saddle-cloth."

4 As Turpin rode over Salisbury Plain
    He met a judge with all his train.
    Then to the judge he did approach
    And robbed him as he sat in his coach.

5 For the shooting of a dunghill cock
    Turpin now at last is took,
    And now he lingers in a jail
    Where his ill-luck he doth bewail.

6 Now Turpin is condemned to die
    And hang upon the gallows high.
    His legacy is the hangman's rope
    For the shooting of a dunghill cock.

traditional

32 High Germany

1   Oh Polly, love, oh Polly,
        the rout it is begun,
    And we must march away
        at the beating of the drum.
    Go dress yourself all in your best
        and come along with me,
    I'll take you to the war, my love,
        in High Germany.

2   Oh Billy, dearest Billy,
        now mind what you do say,
    My feet they are so tender
        I cannot march away.
    Besides, my dearest Billy,
        I am with child by thee,
    Not fitting for the cruel wars
        in High Germany.

3   Cursed by the cruel wars
        that ever they began,
    For they have pressed my Billy
        and many a clever man,
    For they have pressed my Billy
        and all my brothers three
    And sent them to the cruel wars
        in High Germany.

"High" Germany is Southern Germany

traditional

33 The bonnie lass o' Fyvie

1 There was a troop of Irish dragoons
   Came marching down through Fyvie O,
   And their captain fell in love with a handsome
      serving-maid
   And her name it was called pretty Peggy O.

> There's many a bonnie lass in the howe of
>   Auchterless,
> There's many a bonnie lass in the Garioch O,
>   Aberdeen,
> There's many a bonnie Jean in the town o'
> But the flower of them all is in Fyvie O.

2 "Oh, it's come down the stair, pretty Peggy, my dear,
   Come down the stair, pretty Peggy O.
   Oh, come down the stair, comb back your yellow hair,
   Take a last farewell o' your daddy O."

3 "A soldier's wife I never shall be.
   A soldier shall never enjoy me O.
   For I never do intend to go to a foreign land,
   So I never shall marry a soldier O."

4 "A soldier's wife ye never shall be
   For ye'll be the captain's lady O.
   And the regiment shall stand with their hats into
      their hands
   And they'll bow in the presence o' my Peggy O.

5 "It's braw, aye it's braw a captain's lady for to be.
   It's braw to be a captain's lady O.
   It's braw to rant and rove, and to follow at his word,
   And to march when your captain he is ready O."

6 But the Colonel he cries, "Now mount, boys, mount."
   The captain he cries, "Tarry O!
   Oh, gang nae awa' for another day or twa
   Till we see if this bonnie lass will marry O."

7 It was early next morning that we marched away
   And oh, but our captain was sorry O.
   The drums they did beat o'er the bonnie braes o' Gight
   And the band played the Lowlands o' Fyvie O.

8 Long ere we won, into old Meldrum town
   We had our captain to carry O.
   And long ere we won, into bonnie Aberdeen
   We had our captain to bury O.

9 Green grow the birks on bonnie Ythanside
   And low lie the lowlands o' Fyvie O.
   Our captain's name was Ned, and he died for a maid.
   He died for the bonnie lass o' Fyvie O.

howe: area
Auchterless: pronounced Ochterless
Garioch: pronounced Geerie
braw: grand
braes: hills
birk: silver birch
Ythanside: pronounced eye-thanside

traditional

34 John Barleycorn

1　There were three men came out of the west,
　　Their fortunes for to try,
　　And these three men made a solemn vow,
　　John Barleycorn should die.
　　They ploughed, they sowed, they harrowed him in,
　　Throwed clods upon his head,
　　And these three men made a solemn vow,
　　John Barleycorn was dead.

2　Then they let him lie for a very long time
　　Till the rain from heaven did fall,
　　Then little Sir John sprung up his head,
　　And soon amazed them all.
　　They let him stand till midsummer
　　Till he looked both pale and wan,
　　And little Sir John he growed a long beard
　　And so became a man.

3　They hired men with the scythes so sharp
　　To cut him off at the knee,
　　They rolled him and tied him by the waist,
　　And served him most barbarously.
　　They hired men with the sharp pitchforks
　　Who pricked him to the heart,
　　And the loader he served him worse than that,
　　For he bound him to the cart.

4   They wheeled him round and round the field
Till they came unto a barn,
And there they made a solemn mow
Of poor John Barleycorn.
They hired men with the crab-tree sticks
To cut him skin from bone,
And the miller he served him worse than that,
For he ground him between two stones.

5   Here's little Sir John in a nut-brown bowl,
And brandy in a glass;
And little Sir John in the nut-brown bowl
Proved the stronger man at last.
And the huntsman he can't hunt the fox,
Nor so loudly blow his horn,
And the tinker he can't mend kettles or pots
Without a little of Barleycorn.

traditional

35 Casey Jones

1 Come all you rounders, listen here,
   I'll tell you the story of a brave engineer.
   Casey Jones was the hogger's name,
   On a six-eight wheeler, boys, he won his fame.

   Caller called Casey at half-past four,
   He kissed his wife at the station door,
   Mounted to the cabin with his orders in his hand
   And took his farewell trip to the Promised Land.

      Casey Jones! mounted to the cabin,
      Casey Jones! with his orders in his hand,
      Casey Jones! mounted to the cabin
      And took his farewell trip to the Promised Land.

2 Put in your water and shovel in your coal,
   Put your head out the window, watch the drivers roll.
   "I'll run her till she leaves the rail
   'Cause we're eight hours late with the Western Mail."

   He looked at his watch and his watch was slow,
   Looked at the water and the water was low,
   Turned to his fireboy, then he said,
   "We're bound to reach Frisco but we'll all be dead."

      Casey Jones! bound to reach Frisco
      Casey Jones! but we'll all be dead,
      Casey Jones! bound to reach Frisco,
      We're bound to reach Frisco but we'll all be dead.

3   Casey pulled up Reno Hill,
     Tooted at the crossing with an awful shrill.
     "Snakes" all knew by the engine's moans
     That the hogger at the throttle was Casey Jones.

     He pulled up short two miles from the place,
     Freight train stared him straight in the face,
     Turned to his fireboy, "Son, you'd better jump
     'Cause there's two locomotives that are going to bump."

        Casey Jones! two locomotives
        Casey Jones! that are going to bump,
        Casey Jones! two locomotives,
        There's two locomotives that are going to bump.

4   Casey said just before he died,
     "There's two more roads I'd like to ride."
     Fireboy asked, "What can they be?"
     "The Rio Grande and the Santa Fe."

     Mrs Jones sat on her bed a-sigh'n,
     Had a pink that her Casey was dy'n,
     Said, "Hush you children, stop your cry'n
     'Cause you'll get another Papa on the Salt Lake Line."

        Casey Jones! get another Papa
        Casey Jones! on the Salt Lake Line,
        Casey Jones! get another Papa,
        You'll get another Papa on the Salt Lake Line.

T. Lawrence Seibert

36 The Gypsy Davey

1 It was late last night when the squire came home
And asking for his lady.
The only answer that he got,
"She's gone with the Gypsy Davey."

2 "Go saddle me my buckskin horse
And a hundred dollar saddle.
Point out to me their wagon tracks
And after them I'll travel."

3 Well, he had not rode to the midnight moon
When he saw the campfire gleaming.
He heard the noise of the big guitar
And the noise of the gypsies singing.

4 "Have you forsaken your horse and home?
Have you forsaken your baby?
Have you forsaken your husband dear
To go with the Gypsy Davey?"

5 "Yes, I've forsaken my husband dear
To go with the Gypsy Davey,
And I've forsaken my mansion high
But not my blue-eyed baby."

6 "Take off, take off your buckskin gloves
Made of Spanish leather,
Give to me your lily-white hand
And we'll ride home together."

7 "No, I won't take off my buckskin gloves
Made of Spanish leather.
I'll go my way from day to day
And sing with the Gypsy Davey."

traditional

37 The gypsy rover

1   The gypsy rover came over the hill,
Bound for the valley so shady,
He whistled and sang till the greenwoods rang,
And he won the heart of a lady.

> Ah-di-do ah-di-do-da-day,
> Ah-di-do ah-di-day-dee,
> He whistled and sang till the greenwoods rang,
> And he won the heart of a lady.

2   She left her father's castle gate,
She left her own true lover,
She left her servants and her estate
To follow the gypsy rover.
> Ah-di-do ah-di-do-da-day . . .

3   Her father saddled his fastest steed,
Roamed the valley all over,
Sought his daughter at great speed,
And the whistling gypsy rover.
> Ah-di-do ah-di-do-da-day . . .

4   He came at last to a castle gate
Down by the river Claydie,
And there was whisky and there was wine
For the gypsy and his lady.
> Ah-di-do ah-di-do-da-day . . .

5   He is no gypsy, father dear,
But lord of these lands all over,
And I will stay till my dying day
With my whistling gypsy rover.
> Ah-di-do ah-di-do-da-day . . .

Leo Maguire

38 The Ellan Vannin Tragedy

1 Snaefell, Tyn Wald, Ben Mychree,
   Fourteen ships have sailed the sea
   Proudly bearing a Manx name,
   But there's one will never again.

> O Ellan Vannin
> Of the Isle of Man Company,
> O Ellan Vannin,
> Lost in the Irish Sea.

2 At one a.m. in Ramsey Bay
   Captain Tear was heard to say,
   "Our contract says deliver the mail,
   In this rough weather we must not fail."
   O Ellan Vannin . . .

3   Though liners sheltered from the storm,
    Ellan Vannin on the waves was borne.
    Her hold was full and battened down,
    As she sailed on for Liverpool Town.
        O Ellan Vannin . . .

4   Less than a mile from the Bar lightship
    By a mighty wave Ellan Vannin was hit.
    She sank in the waters of Liverpool Bay,
    And there she lies until this day.
        O Ellan Vannin . . .

Hugh Jones

39 Dorset is beautiful

Dorset is beautiful wherever you go,
And the rain in the summertime
    makes the wurzel tree grow.
And it's pleasant to sit
    in the thunder and the hail,
With your girlfriend on a turnip stump
    and hear the sweet nightingale.

1   As I was a-walking one evening in June
    I spied two old farmers making hay in the moon.
    Said one to the other with a twinkle in his eye,
    "There be more birds in the long grass
        than there be in the sky."
        Dorset is beautiful . . .

2   Now Sarah's my girlfriend and I loves her so,
    Her's as big as an 'aystack and forty years old.
    Farmer says she's gi-normous, and loud do he scoff,
    'Cos you has to leave a chalk-mark
        to show where you left off.
        Dorset is beautiful . . .

3   Farmer looks at young Gwendoline and then looks at
        Ned,
    "What an 'andsome young couple, they ought to be wed."
    But then he says sadly, "Tis impossible of course
    'Cos Gwendoline's me daughter and Ned is me horse."
        Dorset is beautiful . . .

4   When Sarah went milking with Nellie the cow
    She pulled and she tugged but she didn't know quite
        how,
    So after a short while Nellie turned with a frown,
    Said "You hang on tight, love, I'll jump up and down."
        Dorset is beautiful . . .

Robert Gale

40 Fling it here, fling it there

1   Way down on our farm we are right up to date,
For mechanisation's the byword of late.
For every task there's a gadget to match,
But our new muck-spreader's the best of the batch.

> Fling it here, fling it there,
> If you're standing by then you'll all get
>   your share.

2   Now young Walter Hodgkins he brought back a load
Of liquid manure from the farm up the road.
He hummed to himself as he drove up the street,
And his load also hummmmmmmed in the afternoon
    heat.
> Fling it here . . .

3   Now this muck-spreader had a mechanical fault,
And a bump in the road turned it on with a jolt.
An odorous spray of manure it let fly
Without fear or favour on all who passed by.
> Fling it here . . .

4   The cats and the dogs stank to high kingdom come,
And the kiddies, browned off, ran home screaming
    to Mum,
The trail of sheer havoc were terrible grim,
One open car were filled up to the brim.
> Fling it here . . .

5   The vicarage windows were all open wide
When a generous helping descended inside.
The vicar, at table, intoned "Let us pray"
When this manure from heaven came flying his way.
> Fling it here . . .

6 In her garden, Miss Pringle was quite scandalised.
"Good gracious!" she cried, "I've been fertilised."
While the Methodist minister's teetotal wife
Were plastered for the very first time in her life.
     Fling it here . . .

7 And all of this time Walter trundled along,
He was quite unaware there was anything wrong,
Till a vision of woe flagged him down ——
   what a sight!
A policeman all covered in . . . you've got it right.
     Fling it here . . .

S. Lawrence/the Yetties

41 Green lanes

Follow the old green lanes.
As the crow flies, so will I.
See how the grey stone walls
Climb the fell and try to touch the sky.

    Farms and cottages
    Clinging to the fellside,
    Far below us and in another world.

Travel the ancient ways
With only sheep to watch you.
See how the water tumbles
Down the fell and disappears from view.

    Come travel with me
    If the spirit moves you.
    Time's an illusion, so leave it far behind.

Follow the old green lanes.
As the crow flies, so will I.
See how the grey stone walls
Climb the fell and try to touch the sky.

Judith Bush

42 Land of the old and grey

1   I am a man of this land,
Thirty long years or more
I have worked the Mallerstang Fells,
Never asked for more.

     Young folks keep moving away,
     Who can get them to stay?
     There's money and there's jobs
       in the wool towns of the valleys.
     This is the land of the old and grey.

2   I have been a leadminer
Over the Swaledale way.
The clothes on your back, they never get dry,
Freezing on a winter's day.
     Young folks keep moving away . . .

3   I have seen the colours of this land,
Thirty long years or more.
Many men drifting to the mines of Durham,
To the Bradford factory floor.
     Young folks keep moving away . . .

4   Working on the Carlisle railway
Mending broken track.
There's snow on the fells and it's raining
   in the valleys,
Muscles aching in my back.
     Young folks keep moving away . . .

Mike Donald

43 If it wasn't for the 'ouses in between

1 If you saw my little backyard,
    "Wot a pretty spot" you'd cry,
  It's a picture on a sunny summer day;
  Wiv the turnip-tops and cabbages
    wot peoples doesn't buy
  I makes it on a Sunday look all gay.
  The neighbours finks I grows 'em
    and you'd fancy you're in Kent,
  Or at Epsom if you gaze into the mews;
  It's a wonder as the landlord
    doesn't want to raise the rent
  Because we've got such nobby distant views.

      Oh! it really is a werry pretty garden,
      And Chingford to the eastward could be seen;
      Wiv a ladder and some glasses,
      You could see to 'Ackney Marshes,
      If it wasn't for the 'ouses in between.

2 We're as countrified as can be
    wiv a clothes-prop for a tree,
  The tub-stool makes a rustic little stile;
  E'vry time the blooming clock strikes
    there's a cuckoo sings to me,
  And I've painted up "To Leather Lane a mile".
  Wiv tomartoes and wiv radishes wot 'adn't any sale,
  The backyard looks a puffick mass o' bloom,
  And I've made a little beehive
    wiv some beetles in a pail,
  And a pitchfork wiv the handle of a broom.

Oh! it really is a werry pretty garden,
And 'Endon to the westward could be seen;
And by clinging to the chimbley,
You could see across to Wembley,
If it wasn't for the 'ouses in between.

3 Though the gas-works isn't wi-lets,
    they improve the rural scene,
For the mountains they would very nicely pass;
There's the mushrooms in the dust-hole
    with the cowcumbers so green
It only wants a bit o' 'ot-'ouse glass.
I wears this milkman's night-shirt,
    and I sits outside all day,
Like the ploughboy cove wot's mizzled o'er the Lea;
And when I goes indoors at night they dunno what I say,
'Cause my language gets as yokel as can be.

Oh! it really is a werry pretty garden,
And soapworks from the 'ouse-tops could be seen;
If I got a rope and pulley
I'd enjoy the breeze more fully,
If it wasn't for the 'ouses in between.

Edgar Bateman

44 The drunken sailor

1 What shall we do with the drunken sailor,
What shall we do with the drunken sailor,
What shall we do with the drunken sailor,
Early in the morning?

     Hooray and up she rises,
     Hooray and up she rises,
     Hooray and up she rises,
     Early in the morning.

2 Put him in the longboat till he's sober . . .

3 Hoist him aboard with a running bowline . . .

4 Put him in the scuppers with a hosepipe on him . . .

5 Pull out the plug and wet him all over . . .

6 Shave his belly with a rusty razor . . .

7 That's what we do with the drunken sailor . . .

traditional (windlass and capstan shanty)

45 Can't you dance the polka

1   As I walked down the Broadway
        one evening in July,
    I met a girl, she asked my trade,
        a sailor John says I.

>   Then away, you Santee, my dear Annie,
>   Oh you New York gals, can't you dance the polka?

2   To Tiffany's I took her,
        I did not mind expense,
    I bought her two gold earrings,
        they cost me fifteen cents.
>   Then away, you Santee, my dear Annie . . .

3   Says she "You Limejuice sailor,
        now see me home you may."
    But when we reached her cottage door,
        she unto me did say,
>   Then away, you Santee, my dear Annie . . .

4   "My flashman he's a Yankee
        with his hair cut short behind,
    He wears a tarry jumper
        and he sails in the Black Ball Line."
>   Then away, you Santee, my dear Annie . . .

traditional (capstan shanty)

46 Haul away Joe

1 Way, haul away, we'll haul away together,
   Way, haul away, we'll haul away Joe,
Way, haul away, we'll haul for better weather,
   Way, haul away, we'll haul away Joe.

2 Now when I was a little lad me mother always told me
   Way, haul away, we'll haul away Joe,
That if I didn't kiss the girls my lips would go
   all mouldy,
   Way, haul away, we'll haul away Joe.

3 Once I had a German girl and she was fat and lazy
And next I had an Irish girl, she damn near drove
   me crazy.

4 King Louis was the king of France before the
   revolution,
King Louis got his head cut off and spoiled his
   constitution.

5 Once I had a scolding wife, she wasn't very civil,
I clapped a plaster on her mouth and sent her
   to the divil.

6 Way, haul away, we'll haul for better weather.
Way, haul away, we'll haul and hang together.

traditional (short-haul shanty)

In shanties like *Haul away Joe* and *Santy Anna* a leader or
shantyman would have sung the first and third lines, with
the rest of the sailors singing the unchanging second and
fourth lines.

47 Santy Anna

1   Oh Santy Anna won the day
      Hooray, Santy Anna!
    And General Taylor ran away
      All on the plains of Mexico.

2   He beat the Prooshans fairly
      Hooray, Santy Anna!
    And whacked the British nearly
      All on the plains of Mexico.

3   He was a rorty general
      Hooray, Santy Anna!
    A rorty snorty general
      All on the plains of Mexico.

4   Twas on the field of Molly del Rey
      Hooray, Santy Anna!
    Santy Anna lost a leg that day
      All on the plains of Mexico.

5   Oh Santy Anna's dead and gone
      Hooray, Santy Anna!
    And all the fighting has been done
      All on the plains of Mexico.

6   So heave away for Mexico
      Hooray, Santy Anna!
    For Mexico where the whalefish blow
      All on the plains of Mexico.

traditional (windlass and capstan shanty)

48 The leaving of Liverpool

1   Fare thee well, the Prince's Landing Stage,
     River Mersey, fare thee well,
     For I'm bound for Californiay,
     A place that I know well.

       So fare thee well, my own true love,
       When I return united we will be.
       It's not the leaving of Liverpool that grieves me
       But darling when I think of thee.

2   Yes I'm bound for Californiay
     By way of the stormy Cape Horn,
     But you know I'll write to you a letter,
     My love, when I am homeward bound.

3   I have signed on a Yankee clipper ship,
     Davy Crockett is her name,
     And her captain's name, it is Burgess,
     And they say she's a floating shame.

4   It's my second trip with Burgess in the *Crockett*,
     And I reckon to know him well.
     If a man is a sailor then he'll be all right,
     But if not, why he's sure in hell.

5   Oh the tug is waiting at the Pier Head
     To take us down the stream,
     Our sails are loose and the anchor is stowed,
     So fare thee well again.

6   Farewell to Lower Frederick Street,
     Anson Terrace and Park Lane,
     For I know that it's going to be a long, long time
     Before I see you again.

traditional

49 The Marco Polo

1   The *Marco Polo*'s a very fine ship,
    The fastest on the sea.
    On Australia's sand we soon will land,
    Bully Forbes can look for me.
    Gonna jump this ship in Melbourne Town,
    Go a-digging gold,
    There's a fortune found beneath the ground
    Where the eucalyptus grow.

    Marco Polo, the fastest on the sea.

2   The Blackball owner Mr. Baines
    Said to Bully Forbes one day
    "It's up to you to keep your crew
    When the gold calls them away."
    Said Bully Forbes to Mr. Baines
    "I have a plan so fine;
    Leave it to me and you'll agree
    I'm the king of the Blackball Line."

    Marco Polo, the fastest on the sea.

3   Now when we reached the Australian shore
    Bully Forbes he made this rule:
    "There's scurvy, boys, so on board you'll stay
    Till we're back in Liverpool."
    And now we lie in the Salthouse Dock,
    I'll go to sea no more.
    I've done my time in the Blackball Line
    Under Captain Bully Forbes.

    Marco Polo, the fastest on the sea.

Hugh Jones

50 The wreck of the John B

1 We come on the sloop *John B*,
   My grandfather and me,
   Round Nassau town we did roam,
   Drinking all night,
   Got into a fight,
   I feel so broke up, I wanna go home.

       So hoist up the *John B*'s sails,
       See how the main-sail sets,
       Send for the captain ashore, let me go home,
       I wanna go home,
       Let me go home,
       I feel so broke up, I wanna go home.

2 The first mate, he got drunk,
   Broke up the people's trunk,
   Constable had to come and take him away.
   Sheriff John Stone,
   Please let me alone,
   I feel so broke up, I wanna go home.
       So hoist up the *John B*'s sails . . .

3 Poor cook he got the fits,
   Throw 'way all the grits,
   Then he took up and eat all o' my corn.
   Let me go home,
   I wanna go home,
   I feel so broke up, I wanna go home.
       So hoist up the *John B*'s sails . . .

traditional

51 Pay me my money down

leader and chorus: Pay me, O pay me,
Pay me my money down,
Pay me or go to jail,
Pay me my money down.

1   **leader:** I thought I heard our Captain say
chorus: Pay me my money down,
leader: Tomorrow is our sailing day.
chorus: Pay me my money down.

leader and chorus: Pay me, O pay me,
Pay me my money down,
Pay me or go to jail,
Pay me my money down.

2   The very next day we crossed the bar,
Pay me my money down,
He hit me on the head with an iron spar.
Pay me my money down.
    Pay me, O pay me . . .

3   I wish I was Mr. Jackson's son,
Pay me my money down,
Sit on the fence and watch work done.
Pay me my money down.
    Pay me, O pay me . . .

traditional

52 Fulera mama

Fulera mama,
> Fulera bechuana bech kago,

Fulera mama,
> Fulera bechuana bech kago,

Fulera,
> Fulera bechuana bech kago,

Kamshikam kono,
> Mfe, Mfwa lundi,

Kamshikam kono,
> Mfe, Mfwa lundi.

Repeat

as sung by Kamau Mwangi and Nganga Mwenja

53 Whip jamboree

1 And now, my lads, be of good cheer,
For the Irish land will soon draw near.
In a few days more we'll sight Cape Clear,
O Jenny get your oat-cake done.

> Whip jamboree, whip jamboree,
> O you pigtailed sailor hanging down behind,
> Whip jamboree, whip jamboree,
> O Jenny get your oat-cake done.

2 And now Cape Clear it is in sight,
We'll be off Holyhead by tomorrow night,
And we'll shape our course for the old Rock Light,
O Jenny get your oat-cake done.
> Whip jamboree, whip jamboree . . .

3 And now, my lads, we're round the Rock,
All hammocks lashed and chests all locked.
We'll haul her into Waterloo dock,
O Jenny get your oat-cake done.
> Whip jamboree, whip jamboree . . .

traditional

54 The Curragh of Kildare

1   The winter it is past
     And the summer's come at last,
     And the birds they are singing in the trees;
     Their little hearts are glad,
     O but mine is very sad,
     For my true love is far away from me.

          And straight I will repair
          To the Curragh of Kildare,
          For it's there I'll find tidings of my dear.

2   A livery I'll wear
     And I'll comb back my hair,
     And in velvet serene I will appear.
          And straight I will repair . . .

3   For you that are in love,
     And it cannot remove,
     I pity the pains that you endure;
     For experience lets me know
     That your hearts are full of woe,
     A wound that no mortal can cure.
          And straight I will repair . . .

traditional

55 The girl I left behind

1   There was a wealthy old farmer
        Who lived in the country nearby,
    He had a lovely daughter
        On whom I cast an eye,
    She was pretty, tall and handsome,
        Indeed, so very fair,
    There was no other girl in the country
        With her I could compare.

2   I asked her if she would be willing
        For me to cross over the plains,
    She said it would make no difference,
        So I returned again,
    She said that she would be true to me
        Till death should prove unkind,
    We kissed and then we parted,
        I left my girl behind.

3   Out in a western city, boys,
        A town we all know well,
    Where everyone was friendly
        And to show me all around,
    Where work and money was plentiful
        And the girls to me proved kind,
    But the only object on my mind
        Was the girl I left behind.

4   As I was rambling around one day
      All down on the public square,
  The mailcoach had arrived
      And I met the mailboy there,
  He handed to me a letter
      That gave me to understand
  That the girl I left in old Texas
      Had married another man.

5   I turned myself all around and about,
      Not knowing what else to do,
  I read on down a piece further
      To see if these words proved true.
  It's drinking I throw over,
      Card-playing I resign,
  For the only girl that I ever loved
      Was the girl I left behind.

6   Come all you rambling gambling boys,
      And listen while I tell,
  Does you no good, kind friends,
      I am sure it will do you no harm,
  If ever you court a fair young maid,
      Just marry her while you can,
  For if ever you cross over the plains,
      She'll marry some other man.

traditional

56 Sweet Willie

1 Come all young girls of a tender mind,
  My story I'll tell to you,
  And listen well to my advice,
  And to my counsel true.

2 As a rule, the mind of a girl is weak
  And the mind of a man is strong,
  And if you listen to what they say
  They're sure to lead you wrong.

3 When I was in my sixteenth year
  Sweet Willie courted me,
  He said if I'd run away with him
  His loving bride I'd be.

4 I love my mother as my life,
  I love my father well,
  But the love I have for sweet Willie dear
  No human tongue can tell.

5 When we were far away from home,
  Enjoying a happy life,
  He said "Go home, go home, little girl,
  For you never can be my wife."

6 "O Willie dear, what have I done?
  What makes you treat me so?
  How can you take me from my home
  And leave me here to mourn?"

7 "It's nature, nature, my little girl,
  I find no fault in you;
  My mind is set on rambling around,
  And now I bid you adieu."

traditional

57 Handsome Molly

1   Wish I was in London
    Or some other seaport town,
    I'd set my foot in a steamboat,
    I'd sail the ocean round.

2   While sailing around the ocean,
    While sailing around the sea,
    I'd think of handsome Molly
    Wherever she might be.

3   She rode to church a-Sunday,
    She passed me on by,
    I saw her mind was changing
    By the roving of her eye.

4   Don't you remember, Molly,
    When you gave me your right hand?
    You said if you ever marry
    That I'd be the man.

5   Now you've broke your promise
    Go marry who you please,
    While my poor heart is aching
    You're lying at your ease.

6   Hair was black as a raven,
    Her eyes were black as coal,
    Her cheeks were like lilies
    That in the morning grow.

7   If I was in London
    Or some other seaport town,
    I'd set my foot in a steamboat,
    I'd sail the ocean round.

traditional

58 The water is wide

1   The water is wide, I cannot get o'er,
     And neither have I wings to fly.
     Give me a boat that will carry two,
     And both shall row, my love and I.

2   Down in the meadow the other day,
     A-gathering flowers both fine and gay,
     A-gathering flowers both red and blue,
     I little thought what love can do.

3   I leaned my back up against an oak,
     Thinking that he was a trusty tree,
     But first he bent and then he broke,
     And so did my false love to me.

4   I put my hand into some soft bush,
     Thinking the fairest flower to find;
     I pricked my finger to the bone,
     But O, I left the rose behind.

5   A ship there is, she sails the seas,
     She's loaded deep as deep can be,
     But not so deep as the love I'm in,
     I know not if I sink or swim.

6   O love is handsome and love is fine
     And love's a jewel while it is new,
     But when it's old it groweth cold
     And fades away like morning dew.

traditional

59 Once I had a sweetheart

1   Once I had a sweetheart but now I have none,
Once I had a sweetheart but now I have none.
He's gone and left me,
He's gone and left me,
He's gone and left me in sorrow to mourn.

2   Last night in sweet slumber I dreamed I did see,
Last night in sweet slumber I dreamed I did see
My own dearest jewel,
My own dearest jewel,
My own dearest jewel sat smiling by me.

3   And when I awakened and found it not so,
And when I awakened and found it not so,
My eyes, like some fountain,
My eyes, like some fountain,
My eyes, like some fountain, with tears overflowed.

4   I'll set sail for Dublin, for France and for Spain,
I'll set sail for Dublin, for France and for Spain
In hopes for to meet,
In hopes for to meet,
In hopes for to meet my dear jewel again.

traditional

60 Liverpool Lou

O Liverpool Lou, lovely Liverpool Lou,
Why don't you behave just like other girls do?
Why must my poor heart keep following you?
Stay home and love me, my Liverpool Lou.

1 When I go a-walking
   I hear people talking,
   School children playing,
   I know what they're saying,
   They're saying you'll grieve me,
   That you will deceive me,
   Some morning you'll leave me,
   All packed up and gone.
       O Liverpool Lou, lovely Liverpool Lou . . .

2 The sounds from the river
   Keep telling me ever
   That I should forget you
   Like I'd never met you.
   O tell me the song, love,
   Was never more wrong, love,
   Please say I belong, love,
   To my Liverpool Lou.
       O Liverpool Lou, lovely Liverpool Lou . . .

Dominic Behan

61 The orchestra song

violins: The violins of all the strings
We take the lead and have the most to do.
We gaily play the melody
And sing away the whole piece through.

clarinets: The clarinet, the clarinet
Of all the woodwind we most notes can get.
A single reed is all we need
To make our smooth and mellow sound.

horns: The horns, the horns
Of curling brass
Can murmur low
Or loudly blast.

trumpets: For the fanfare our trumpety sound is best,
Our trumpety sound is best, our trumpety
sound is best.
For the fanfare our trumpety sound is best,
Our trumpety sound is best, is best!

drums: The kettle drums echo
The two notes we best know:
Soh, doh, doh soh,
Soh soh soh soh doh.

John Hosier

62 I'm not strong, Sir

I'm not strong, Sir,
Sure, 'tis wrong, Sir,
Such high notes my voice do strain.

I can't sing a note, Sir,
Something hurts my throat, Sir,
Though I try my best, 'tis all in vain.

I'm quite hoarse, Sir,
So, of course, Sir,
I cannot sing this round again.

63 Have you seen the ghost of Tom?

Have you seen the ghost of Tom?
Long white bones with the rest all gone,
Oooooooooooooooooooooh,
Wouldn't it be chilly with no skin on?

64 Whose pigs are these?

Whose pigs are these?
Whose pigs are these?
They are John Potts', you can tell 'em by the spots,
And I found 'em in the vicarage garden.

65 The barmaid in Sale

On the chest of a barmaid in Sale
Were tattooed all the prices of ale,
And on her behind,
For the sake of the blind,
Was the very same list in braille.

66 Lady Madonna

1   Lady Madonna, children at your feet,
     Wonder how you manage to make ends meet;
     Who finds the money when you pay the rent?
     Did you think that money was heaven sent?
         Friday night arrives without a suitcase,
         Sunday morning creeping like a nun,
         Monday's child has learned to tie his bootlace,
         See how they run.

2   Lady Madonna, baby at your breast,
     Wonder how you manage to feed the rest.
     Lady Madonna, lying on the bed,
     Listen to the music playing in your head.
         Tuesday afternoon is never-ending,
         Wednesday morning papers didn't come,
         Thursday night your stockings needed mending,
         See how they run.

     Lady Madonna, children at your feet,
     Wonder how you manage to make ends meet.

John Lennon and Paul MacCartney

67 Penny Lane

1   In Penny Lane there is a barber showing photographs
     Of every head he's had the pleasure to know,
     And all the people that come and go
     Stop and say "hello".

2 On the corner is a banker with a motor car,
The little children laugh at him behind his back,
And the banker never wears a mac
In the pouring rain.
Very strange.

> Penny Lane is in my ears and in my eyes.
> There beneath the blue suburban skies I sit, and
> Meanwhile, back

3 In Penny Lane there is a fireman with an hour-glass,
And in his pocket is a portrait of the Queen.
He likes to keep his fire-engine clean,
It's a clean machine.

> Penny Lane is in my ears and in my eyes.
> A four of fish and finger pies in summer.
> Meanwhile, back

4 Behind the shelter in the middle of the roundabout
The pretty nurse is selling poppies from a tray.
And though she feels as if she's in a play,
She is anyway.

5 In Penny Lane the barber shaves another customer,
We see the banker sitting waiting for a trim,
And then the fireman rushes in
From the pouring rain.
Very strange.

> Penny Lane is in my ears and in my eyes.
> There beneath the blue suburban skies I sit, and
> Meanwhile back,
> Penny Lane is in my ears and in my eyes.
> There beneath the blue suburban skies,
> Penny Lane.

John Lennon and Paul MacCartney

68 The windmills of your mind

Round like a circle in a spiral,
    like a wheel within a wheel,
Never ending or beginning
    on an ever spinning reel,
Like a snowball down a mountain,
    or a carnival balloon,
Like a carousel that's turning
    running rings around the moon,
Like a clock whose hands are sweeping
    past the minutes of its face,
And the world is like an apple
    whirling silently in space,
Like the circles that you find
    in the windmills of your mind.

Like a tunnel that you follow
    to a tunnel of its own,
Down a hollow to a cavern
    where the sun has never shone,
Like a door that keeps revolving
    in a half-forgotten dream,
Or the ripples from a pebble
    someone tosses in a stream,
Like a clock whose hands are sweeping
    past the minutes of its face,
And the world is like an apple
    whirling silently in space,
Like the circles that you find
    in the windmills of your mind.

Keys that jingle in your pocket,
   words that jangle in your head,
Why did summer go so quickly?
   Was it something that you said?
Lovers walk along a shore
   and leave their footprints in the sand,
Is the sound of distant drumming
   just the fingers of your hand?
Pictures hanging in a hallway
   and the fragment of a song,
Half-remembered names and faces,
   but to whom do they belong?
When you knew that it was over
   you were suddenly aware
That the autumn leaves were turning
   to the colour of her hair.

Like a circle in a spiral,
   like a wheel within a wheel,
Never ending or beginning
   on an ever spinning reel,
As the images unwind,
Like the circles that you find
In the windmills of your mind.

Marilyn and Alan Bergman

69 An Eriskay love lilt

Vair me oro van o,
Vair me oro van ee,
Vair me oru o ho,
Sad am I without thee.

1 When I'm lonely, dear white heart,
Black the night, or wild the sea,
By love's light my foot finds
The old pathway to thee.
    Vair me oro van o . . .

2 Thou'rt the music of my heart,
Harp of joy, oh cruit mo chridh,
Moon of guidance by night,
Strength and light thou'rt to me.
    Vair me oro van o . . .

cruit mo chridh: harp of my heart, pronounced "crootch mo chree".

English adaptation by Marjory Kennedy-Fraser

70 Sailing

1 I am sailing, I am sailing,
   Home again, 'cross the sea.
   I am sailing stormy waters
   To be near you, to be free.

2 I am flying, I am flying,
   Like a bird, 'cross the sky.
   I am flying, passing high clouds,
   To be with you, to be free.

3 Can you hear me, can you hear me
   Through the dark night far away?
   I am dying, forever trying
   To be with you, who can say?

4 We are sailing, we are sailing
   Home again 'cross the sea.
   We are sailing stormy waters
   To be near you, to be free.

Gavin Sutherland

71 The yellow rose of Texas

1   There's a yellow rose in Texas
That I am going to see,
Nobody else can have her,
Nobody, only me.
She cried so when I left her,
It nearly broke my heart,
And if I ever find her
We never more will part.

>She's the sweetest little rosebud
>That Texas ever knew,
>Her eyes are bright as diamonds,
>They sparkle like the dew.
>You can talk about your dearest May
>And sing of Rosa Lee,
>But the yellow rose of Texas
>Is the only girl for me.

2   Where the Rio Grande is flowing
And the starry skies are bright,
She walks along the river
In the quiet summer night;
She thinks, if I remember,
When we parted long ago,
I promised to come back again
And not to leave her so.
>She's the sweetest little rosebud . . .

3 O now I'm going to find her,
 For my heart is full of woe;
 We'll sing the songs together
 We sang so long ago;
 We'll play the banjo gaily
 And sing the songs of yore,
 And the yellow rose of Texas
 Will be mine for evermore.
     She's the sweetest little rosebud . . .

72 Messing about on the river

1 When the weather is fine then you know it's a sign
   For messing about on the river.
   If you take my advice, there's nothing so nice
   As messing about on the river.
      There are long boats and short boats and all sorts
         of craft,
         And cruisers and keel boats and some with no draught.
   So take off your coat and hop in a boat,
   Go messing about on the river.

2 There are boats made from kits that reach you in bits,
   For messing about on the river,
   Or you might like to scull in a fibre-glass hull,
   Just messing about on the river.
      There are tillers and rudders and anchors and cleats,
         And ropes that are sometimes referred to as sheets.
   With the wind in your face, there's no finer place
   Than messing about on the river.

3   There are skippers and mates, and rowing club eights,
Just messing about on the river.
There are pontoons and trots, and all sorts of knots,
For messing about on the river.
   With inboards and outboards and dinghies you sail,
   The first thing you learn is the right way to bail.
In a one-seat canoe you're skipper and crew,
Just messing about on the river.

4   There are bridges and locks and moorings and docks
When messing about on the river.
There's a whirlpool and weir that you mustn't go near
When messing about on the river.
   There are back-water places all hidden from view,
   And quaint little islands just waiting for you,
So I'll leave you right now to cast off your bow,
To go messing about on the river.

Tony Hatch

73 The lightning tree

1 Down in the meadow where the wind blows free,
   In the middle of a field stands the lightning tree,
   Its limbs all torn from the day it was born,
   For the tree was born in a thunderstorm.
   > Grow, grow the lightning tree,
   > It's never too late for you and me,
   > Grow, grow the lightning tree,
   > Never give in too easily.

2 Down in the meadow where the wind blows light,
   The lightning struck in the middle of the night,
   Its limbs stripped bare by the lightning flare,
   The lightning flare was a wild affair.
   > Grow, grow the lightning tree,
   > It's never too late for you and me,
   > Grow, grow the lightning tree,
   > Never give in too easily.

3 Down in the valley where the wind blows cold,
   The lightning tree stands stiff and old,
   Branches bent when the lightning rent,
   The lightning rent from the firmament.
   > Grow, grow the lightning tree,
   > Never give in too easily.

4 Down in the meadow with the wind in the west,
   The lightning tree faced up to the test,
   Its heart went snap when it took the rap,
   The terrible rap of the thunder clap.
   > Grow, grow the lightning tree,
   > It's never too late for you and me,
   > Grow, grow the lightning tree,
   > Never give in too easily.

5   Down in the valley where the wind blows free,
    A whisper of green in the lightning tree,
    Dreams come true when you want them to,
    If you want them to then it's up to you.
        Grow, grow the lightning tree,
        Never give in too easily.
        Grow, grow the lightning tree,
        It's never too late for you and me,
        Grow, grow the lightning tree,
        Never give in too easily.

Stephen Francis

74 I can see for miles

I know you've deceived me, now here's a surprise:
I know that you have 'cos there's magic in my eyes,
I can see for miles and miles and miles and miles
    and miles, oh yeah.

1 If you think that I don't know about the little
    tricks you play,
  And never see you when deliberately you put things
    in my way,
  Well here's a poke at you,
  You're gonna choke on it too.
  You're gonna lose that smile,
  Because all the while
      I could see for miles and miles,
      I could see for miles and miles,
      I can see for miles and miles and miles and
        miles and miles, oh yeah.

2 You took advantage of my trust in you when I was so
    far away,
  I saw you holding lots of other guys and now you
    got the nerve to say
  That you still want me.
  Well, that's as may be,
  But you gotta stand trial,
  Because all the while
      I could see for miles and miles,
      I could see for miles and miles,
      I can see for miles and miles and miles and
        miles and miles, oh yeah.

3   The Eiffel Tower and the Taj Mahal are mine to see
        on clear days.
    You thought that I would need a crystal ball to
        see right through the haze.
    Well here's a poke at you,
    You're gonna choke on it too.
    You're gonna lose that smile,
    Because all the while
            I could see for miles and miles,
            I could see for miles and miles,
            I can see for miles and miles and miles and
                miles and miles and miles and miles and miles.

Peter Townshend

75 Scarborough Fair

1   Are you going to Scarborough Fair?
      Parsley, sage, rosemary and thyme
   Remember me to one who lives there,
   She once was a true love of mine.

2   Tell her to make me a cambric shirt
      Parsley, sage, rosemary and thyme
   Without any seam or needlework,
   Then she'll be a true love of mine.

3   Tell her to wash it in yonder dry well
      Parsley, sage, rosemary and thyme
   Where water ne'er sprung, nor drop of rain fell,
   Then she'll be a true love of mine.

4   Tell her to dry it on yonder thorn
      Parsley, sage, rosemary and thyme
   Which never bore blossom since Adam was born,
   Then she'll be a true love of mine.

5   Are you going to Scarborough Fair?
      Parsley, sage, rosemary and thyme
   Remember me to one who lives there,
   She once was a true love of mine.

traditional

76 The wild mountain thyme

1 O the summer-time is coming,
   And the trees are sweetly blooming,
   And the wild mountain thyme
   Grows around the blooming heather.

>   Will ye go, lassie, go,
>   And we'll all go together
>   To pull wild mountain thyme
>   All around the blooming heather,
>   Will ye go, lassie, go.

2 I will build my love a tower
   Near yon pure crystal fountain,
   And on it I will build
   All the flowers of the mountain.
   >   Will ye go, lassie, go . . .

3 If my true love she were gone
   I would surely find another,
   Where wild mountain thyme
   Grows around the blooming heather.
   >   Will ye go, lassie, go . . .

Francis McPeake

77 Thank U very much

1 Thank u very much for the Aintree Iron,
   Thank u very much, thank u very very very much,
   Thank u very much for the Aintree Iron,
   Thank u very very very much.

2 Thank u very much for the birds and bees,
   Thank u very much, thank u very very very much,
   Thank u very much for the birds and bees,
   Thank u very very very much.

3 Thank u very much for the family circle,
   Thank u very much, thank u very very very much,
   Thank u very much for the family circle,
   Thank u very very very much.

4 Thank u very much for . . (*spoken*) love,
   Thank u very much, thank u very very very much,
   Thank u very much for . . (*spoken*) love,
   Thank u very very very much.

5 Thank u very much for the Sunday joint,
   Thank u very much, thank u very very very much,
   Thank u very much for the Sunday joint,
   And our cultural heritage, national beverage,
   Being fat, Union Jack,
   Nursery rhymes, Sunday Times . . .
   Thank u very much, thank u very very very very
      very very very very much.

6 Thank u very much for buying this song book,
   Thank u very much, thank u very very very much,
   Thank u very much for buying this song book,
   Thank u very very very much.

7 Thank u very much for our gracious team,
 Thank u very much, thank u very very very much,
 Thank u very much for our gracious team,
 Thank u very much, thank u very very very very
 very very very very . . (*spoken*) much.

Michael McGear

Acknowledgements

Grateful acknowledgement is made to the following who have granted permission for the reprinting of copyright material:

Boosey & Hawkes Music Publishers Ltd for 69 'An Eriskay love lilt', © 1909 Boosey & Co Ltd, reprinted from *Songs of the Hebrides* by permission of the Estate of M. Kennedy Fraser and Boosey & Hawkes Music Publishers Ltd.

Box & Cox Publications for 37 'The gypsy rover' by Leo Maguire.

Sydney Bron Music Co Ltd for 18 'Across the hills' by Leon Rosselson, 21 'My last cigarette' by Sydney Carter and 22 'I'm the urban spaceman' by Neil Innes.

Judith Bush for 41 'Green lanes'

CPP/Belwin Europe for 20 'Air' (Rado/Ragni/MacDermot) © 1966, 1967, 1968 EMI Catalogue Partnership/EMI Unart Catalog Inc, USA and 68 'The windmills of your mind' (Allan and Marilyn Bergman/Michel Legrand) © 1968 EMI Catalogue Partnership/EMI U Catalog Inc, USA; Reprinted by permission of CPP/Belwin Europe, Surrey, England.

Crown Publishers Inc for 19 'Pollution' by Tom Lehrer, from *Tom Lehrer's Second Song Book*.

Dejamus Ltd for 72 'Messing about on the river' composed by Tony Hatch © 1960 Dejamus Music Ltd.

Durham Music Co Ltd for 17 'Leave them a flower' (words only) by Wally Whyton © 1969/70 Durham Music Ltd, 1a Farm Place, London W8 7SX.

Early Morning Music USA for 16 'Cotton Jenny' by Gordon Lightfoot © Reprinted by permission of Campbell Connelly & Co Ltd 8-9 Frith Street London W1V 5TZ.

Ted Edwards for 9 'Coal-hole cavalry' © Ted Edwards.

EFDS Publications Ltd for 8 'Settle Carlisle railway', 11 'The broadside man' and 42 'Land of the old and grey all © 1970 EFDS Publications Ltd; and for 14 'Bob the pedigree sheepdog' © 1974 EFDS Publications Ltd.

EMI Music Publishing Ltd for 24 'Where did you get that hat?', © 1890 Francis Day & Hunter Ltd, 25 'The Field of the Willows', © 1969 Robbins Music Corp Ltd, and 43 'If it wasn't for the 'ouses in between', © 1894 Francis Day & Hunter Ltd.

Fabulous Music Ltd for 74 'I can see for miles', by Peter Townshend © Fabulous Music Ltd.

Folktracks and Soundpost Publications, The Centre for Oral Traditions, Grapevine House, Harberton, Totnes, Devon, for 39 'Dorset is beautiful' words by Robert Gale.

Harmony Music Ltd for 7 'Indeed I would' (words only) by Ewan MacColl © 1966 Harmony Music Ltd, and for Marco Polo (words only) by Hugh Jones © 1964 Harmony Music Ltd, 1a Farm Place, London W8 7SX.

David Higham Associates Ltd for 12 'Timothy Winters' and 23 'Colonel Fazackerley': words by Charles Causley.

John Hosier and Voggenreiter Verlag for 61 'The orchestra song'.

International Music Publishers Limited for 76 'Wild Mountain Thyme' words and music by The McPeake Family Trio © 1962 EFDS Publications Ltd, Chappell Music Ltd, London W1Y 3FA. Reproduced by permission.

Island Music Ltd for 70 'Sailing' by Gavin Sutherland © 1972 Island Music Ltd.

Logo Songs Ltd for 3 'The gulls o' Invergordon' © Heathside Music Ltd/Logo Songs Ltd, and 26 'Mole in a hole', by Mike Waterson © 1974 Leading Note Ltd.

Maypole Music Ltd for 40 'Fling it here, fling it there' by S. Lawrence/the Yetties.

Mockbeggar Music, 24 Beresford Road, Wallasey, Merseyside L45 0JJ, for 38 'The Ellan Vannin tragedy', by Hugh Jones © Mockbeggar Music.

Music Sales Ltd for 66 'Lady Madonna', © 1968 Northern Songs for the world, and 67 'Penny Lane' © 1967 Northern Songs for the world.

Noel Gay Music Co Ltd for 4 'Right said Fred' (Dicks, Rudge), 5 'Hole in the ground' (Dicks, Rudge) and 77 'Thank U very much' (McGear), all © Noel Gay Music Co Ltd, and for 13 'Pete was a lonely mongrel dog who lived in central Wigan (Lancs)' by John Meeks, Colin Radcliffe Copyright © Wednesday Music Ltd.

Simon & Schuster for 63 'Have you seen the ghost of Tom?', from *The Fireside Book of Children's Songs* by Marie Winn, © 1966 Marie Winn and Alan Miller.

Television Music Ltd for 73 'The lightning tree' by Stephen Francis.

Wildwood Music Ltd for 60 'Liverpool Lou' by Dominic Behan © 1965 and 1974 Wildwood Music.

World Around Songs (Burnsville, N.C. 28714) for 52 'Fulera Mama', © 1958.

Every effort has been made to trace and acknowledge copyright owners. If any right has been omitted the publishers offer their apologies and will rectify this in subsequent editions following notification.

Index of titles and first lines

First lines are printed like this, *titles are printed like this.*